Healthy Cooking for One

Mari Hills

Note for Librarians: a cataloguing record for this book that includes Dewey Classification and US Library of Congress numbers is available from the National Library of Canada. The complete cataloguing record can be obtained from the National Library's online database at: www.nlc-bnc.ca/amicus/index-e.html

ISBN 1-4120-1592-8

TRAFFORD

This book was published on-demand in cooperation with Trafford Publishing.
On-demand publishing is a unique process and service of making a book available for retail sale to the public taking advantage of on-demand manufacturing and Internet marketing. On-demand publishing includes promotions, retail sales, manufacturing, order fulfilment, accounting and collecting royalties on behalf of the author.

Suite 6E, 2333 Government St., Victoria, B.C. V8T 4P4, CANADA

Phone	250-383-6864	Toll-free	1-888-232-4444 (Canada & US)
Fax	250-383-6804	E-mail	sales@trafford.com

Web site www.trafford.com   TRAFFORD PUBLISHING IS A DIVISION OF TRAFFORD HOLDINGS LTD.
Trafford Catalogue #03-1969   www.trafford.com/robots/03-1969.html

10   9   8   7   6   5   4   3   2   1

This is my first book, I would not have written it without the inspiration and motivation of my son.

Dennis, I love you always.

Photography: Mary Hills

About This Book

This book is intended to be a useful cluster of quick and simple recipes. All made with common ingredients and fresh products available in most grocery stores. In Healthy Cooking for One, each dish has been designed to serve one in style.

Fast food restaurants are not in my favorite list as they are mostly high on fats, carbohydrates and calories; while fast food restaurants offer biggie sizes, I prefer the small sizes. When you talk about eating well, size matters. I like to cook my own food, being fresh, tasty and having control of the serving portion and the amount of fats that I intake. Even I have a full time job; I prefer to dedicate a short time to prepare my own meals looking for tasty and fast recipes that allows me some evening time for myself, while eating well. Long cooking projects are being left for another book; this one is dedicated to those after-work early-evening meals and snacks full of taste in a short time.

Being a single mom demands to cook in small portions and minimize leftovers. Unlike others who might prefer to cook large amounts and leave leftovers for next day, I rather cook less quantity of food and have minimum leftovers. For my taste, freshly prepared food…just taste better.

I choose fresh products, roots, fruits and vegetables. My favorite dishes go from sandwiches, dips, salads to stir fries, all with a potpourri of different flavors.
In this book you will find recipes that I have prepared for a long time. You'll see that garlic, olive oil, cilantro and spices are in most of my recipes.

If you are looking for ideas to prepare quick, tasty dishes, in single portions…this book is for you.

Tips and Ideas

Meats, Beef, Chicken and Fish

• Right amount, always handy: As soon as I get home from the grocery store, I take advantage that meat/beef/chicken/fish is thawed to divide it into single portions. Then slightly season it, put it into zippered plastic bags and freeze; this way you only need to unfreeze the amount you want to cook.

• It is easier to slice beef, meat or chicken breasts if you put them in the freezer for about ½ hour.

• To prevent bacteria, defrost sealed frozen food in the refrigerator on a plate instead of on the kitchen counter.

Seasonings

• Prepare your Mari's Home-Made Seasoning, keep one small portion in the fridge in a sealed container, enough for 1-2 weeks; the rest can be frozen in an ice-cube tray; once frozen, you may pop them into a zippered plastic bag. This will avoid odor spread into the other food in the freezer, while having handy individual portions.

• For Home-Made Seasoning, see Mari's Home-Made Seasoning recipe in this book.

• Mix your favorite dry herbs and spices and have it handy to shake over food.

Ideas

• Zippered plastic bags – convenient to keep food in fridge or freezer; space-saver; see-through; re-usable (wash well before re-use).

• Ice-cube tray – great for freezing seasoning & small portion of sauces.

• Mortar – great to crush garlic & spices

• When cooking rice, add a cube of chicken or beef broth to the water

• When you beat food with an electric or hand mixer, always use a large bowl to prevent splatters. Locate mixing bowl in the clean sink, and just wash sink out when done.

• To thicken soups, add a little of instant potato flakes, or add a slice of potato very finely chopped.

• To crush garlic in a mortar, add a bit of salt and pepper before crushing

• Add shredded parmesan or cheddar cheese, cilantro and crushed garlic to mashed potatoes

• Refrigerate fresh cilantro wrapping the roots with a slightly wet paper towel in a plastic bag.

• To prepare herbs-butter, leave butter at room temperature to soften, and then add crushed garlic and herbs. Put back into refrigerator.

More Ideas...

• Soften ice cream at room temperature; add small chunks of fruits; blend and re-freeze.

• If you are counting calories, substitute ingredients with low-fat or low-sugar.

• Add or change spices as you like, be creative in adding those you like most.

• When cooking pasta, do not add oil to the water, oil will not allow sauces to stick well to the pasta.

• To keep the ice cream from getting crystals, cover it with plastic wrap before putting the lid back on.

• It is easier to cut soft cheeses, such as mozzarella or goat cheese, if you put them in the freezer for a couple of minutes before cutting.

• To speed ripening of an avocado, put it in a dry dark place (for example, kitchen cabinet or unused oven) for a couple of days. Check daily for ripening, avocado skin will not change color while ripening, but it's soft to the touch.

• Keep cut apples, bananas and avocado from browning by squeezing a few drops of fresh lemon juice on them.

• Save counter space by removing all those small appliances that you don't frequently use.

• Organize your refrigerator by grouping like items together. Place all beverages on the same shelf. Place all fruits on same shelf.

• Use see-through plastic bags and containers; you will always know what's inside.

More Ideas...

• Storage cereal, flour, pasta, etc in clear (see-through) containers. Stack the containers in your cabinet or pantry and save space by using square containers, these will take up less space than rounded ones.

• If you have a plant in the kitchen, locate it next to the sink, you won't forget to water it.

• To get more juice out of the lemons, roll them under your palm against the kitchen counter before cutting and squeezing.

• To remove stuck food from the skillet, add soapy water and bring to a boil. It will be much easier to clean.

• Use low-fat or regular ingredients based on your eating habits.

• If tomatoes are too ripened, puree them into tomato sauce or dips

• Top your soups with avocado, finely chopped.

• Kitchen Ergonomics: keep utensils near your stove, keep dishes near the dishwasher, keep seasonings near the cooking area, keep working area near the stove/oven, good lighting, prepare ingredients beforehand.

• Add several slices of lemon and/or orange to a pitcher of cold water.

• For single recipes, more convenient (prevent leftovers) if you buy grape, cherry or plum tomatoes. Perfect size for small portions. For recipes, use the ones you most prefer adjusting the amount required for the recipe.

• Fresh fruits and vegetables don't last long; estimate what you really consume in a week and buy only that amount.

And Some More Ideas...

• Save in paper towels, have some hand towels instead.

• Don't go to the grocery store in a rush; take your time to read the labels!

• To prevent ice-cream to stick to scoop, wet the ice-cream scoop in warm water before every scoop.

• Crack eggs in a separate bowl one by one before you add them to the mix, this way you'll avoid any rotten egg to spoil the mix.

• To prevent bacteria spread, use one separate cutting board only for poultry and meats.

• To prevent lettuce leaves from browning, don't cut them with a knife, use your hands instead.

• Read recipes before you start; make sure you have all ingredients (or substitutes), utensils and appliances before you start.

• Pierce a potato a few times before baking to allow steam to escape. Once baked, use a knife to cut along the top, and squeeze to gently fluff (careful if too hot).

• Adjust amount of ingredients based on your taste, if you love tomatoes, why not add a little bit more?

• If you don't like a vegetable or greens in a recipe... replace it with one you like (sweet potato for potato; spinach for lettuce).

Contents

Quick and Easy...

Dressings & Seasonings

Mari's Homemade Seasoning

Mari's Homemade Seasoning

Serves: 1
Cooking Time: 0 Minutes
Total Time: 10 Minutes

1 large red onion, sliced
1 green bell pepper, sliced (no seeds)
1 yellow or orange green pepper, sliced (no seeds) – this will add color
2-3 oz fresh cilantro
5-6 oz garlic, peeled
4-5 tsp olive oil
salt and black/red pepper – to taste (about 1/8 tsp each)

Wash cilantro in fresh water, drain.

In a food processor, chop or mince all ingredients. It will take only a few seconds. If you prefer to leave small chunks, manually pulse until mix is smooth, about 15 times. Mince mix until desired consistency and chunks size.

Pour mix into plastic or glass container, tightly closed, and keep in the refrigerator. It will last for several weeks, with same great taste. If desired, you also can pour seasoning mix into ice-cube tray, freeze; and then pop up cubes as needed.

Serving suggestion: Add 1-2 tsp when cooking soups, stews, and stir-fries.

Note: if you like it chili hot, you may add 1 small chili pepper or a few drops of hot oil into the mix during blending.

Vinaigrette Salad Dressing

Serves: 1
Cooking Time: 0 Minutes
Total Time: 5 Minutes

¼ cup olive oil
⅛ cup garlic vinegar
salt & pepper
a few leaves cilantro, finely chopped
1 garlic, minced or mashed
juice from ½ lemon

In a blender, mix all ingredients.

Refrigerate.

Note: great on green salads.

Salad Dressing

Serves: 1
Cooking Time: 0 Minutes
Total Time: 5 Minutes

¼ cup olive oil
⅛ cup white vinegar
1 tsp sugar
2 tsp parmesan cheese, grated
1 garlic, minced or mashed
a few fresh cilantro leaves, finely chopped

Mix all ingredients and shake well.

Keep refrigerated until use.

Great on green salads.

Avocado Dressing

Serves: 1
Cooking Time: 0 Minutes
Total Time: 5 Minutes

10 tsp olive oil
½ avocado (3-4 oz)
1 clove garlic, mashed
salt and pepper to taste
a few leaves cilantro
1-2 slices tomato, chopped
a few drops of fresh lemon juice

Blend all ingredients for a few seconds. It will be a get a slightly thick consistency. Check for chunk sizes or totally puree the mix, to your taste.

Keep it simple…

Wraps & Sandwiches

Spinach Quesadillas

Serves: 1
Cooking Time: 2 Minutes
Total Time: 5 Minutes

2 fajita size tortillas
a few leaves spinach, finely chopped
2-3 tbsp cream cheese, softened
1 slice red onion, finely chopped
a few leaves cilantro, finely chopped

In a griddle or non-stick skillet, warm tortillas at low heat, about 30 seconds each side. Set aside.

Mix all the other ingredients.

Spread mix over one tortilla, cover with the other one.

Broil in toaster oven until slightly golden.

Cut into wedges.

Serve with a salsa dip.

Egg Sandwich

Serves: 1
Cooking Time: 0 Minutes
Total Time: 5 Minutes

2 eggs, cooked hard-boiled, peeled
2 tsp low-fat mayonnaise
salt & pepper, to taste
1 tsp green onions, finely sliced
cajun pepper, to taste

french bread cut in half
1 thin slice avocado

Mash eggs and add the rest of the ingredients (except avocado and bread).

Broil bread in toaster oven until lightly toasted. Remove immediately.

Spread egg mix over french bread.

Top with avocado.

Serve

King Crab Sandwich

Serves: 1
Cooking Time: 0 Minutes
Total Time: 5 Minutes

½ cup king crab meat, cooked, shredded
2 tsp low-fat mayonnaise
2 tsp cream cheese, softened
a few leaves cilantro, finely chopped
salt & pepper, to taste
1 tsp green onions, finely sliced
1 tsp red onions, finely chopped

french bread, cut in half
2 slices plum tomato

Broil bread in toaster oven until lightly toasted. Remove immediately.

Mix all the rest of ingredients (except tomato) and spread over bread.

Top with tomato slices.

Hints: Also great on top of toasts or crackers
        For a spicy flavor, you may use hot mayonnaise

Caribbean Sandwich

Caribbean Sandwich

Serves: 1
Cooking Time: 0 Minutes
Total Time: 10 Minutes

french bread

Filling ingredients:
½ small avocado, chopped (1-2 oz)
1 clove garlic, crushed or minced
1 slice red onions, chopped   (2 tsp)
4-5 leaves of baby spinach, chopped
1-2 oz cooked turkey ham or turkey pastrami, finely chopped
2 tsp olive oil
2 tsp ketchup
1 slice plum tomato, chopped
a pinch of salt and pepper

Mix all ingredients.

Let it stand by a couple of minutes to blend flavors.

Cut french bread (sandwich style & size); spread filling mix.

Serving suggestion: During hot summer days, taste even better if you cool the filling mix for a few minutes in the refrigerator.

Tuna Salad Wraps

Tuna Salad Wraps

Serves: 1
Cooking Time: 0 Minutes
Total Time: 5 Minutes

2-3 oz white tuna, packed in water, drained
1 leaf lettuce and/or a few leaves of spinach
a few leaves fresh cilantro, chopped
1 tsp green onions, chopped
1 tsp red onions, chopped
a few drops of fresh lemon juice
a pinch of red pepper (to taste)
a pinch of dry seasonings
1 tsp low-fat mayonnaise
3-4 grape tomatoes, sliced (or 1 slice plum tomato, chopped)
2 thin slices avocado
1 tortilla wrap (flour tortilla, soft taco style)

In a medium bowl, combine mayonnaise, seasonings, lemon juice, green and red onions.

Warm tortillas in microwave for about 20 seconds.

Stuff tortilla with lettuce, spinach, tomatoes, tuna mix, cilantro, avocado.

Wrap around and Serve.

Pesto Toasts

Serves: 1
Cooking Time: 0 Minutes
Total Time: 5 Minutes

2 tsp pesto spread
1 tbsp olive oil
1 small plum tomato, thinly sliced
parmesan cheese, thinly sliced
french bread
a few leaves cilantro, finely chopped
1 clove of garlic, minced or mashed
fresh juice from ½ lemon

Cut french bread in diagonal slices ½ inch thick; slightly toast it in toaster oven.

Mix cilantro, pesto, olive oil, lemon juice and garlic.

Spread the pesto mix on toasts, top with tomato and cheese.

Put back in toaster for a few seconds to slightly melt the cheese.

Remove and serve immediately.

Discover plantain…

Plantains

Plantains are similar to bananas, but larger. They are starchy rather than sweet, and a source of potassium and vitamin c. They are cooked in same way of potatoes; you may bake, broil, fry or boil them. If kept at room temperature, they ripe very slowly. Cook while still green, once skin turns yellow/brown, they taste sweeter; they are softer and can be eaten raw.

How to peel a plantain: using a knife, cut ends first, then make a long shallow cut lengthwise and remove the skin.

Fried Plantain

Serves: 1
Cooking Time: 2 Minutes
Total Time: 5 Minutes

1 large green plantain
vegetable or olive oil for frying
salt to taste

In a medium size frying pan, heat oil at medium heat.

Peel plantain, cut in diagonal thin slices.

Fry in oil for about 1 minute each side or until slightly brown and crisp.

Remove and drain in paper towel.

Sprinkle salt or your preferred dry seasoning.

Plantain Soup

Serves: 1
Cooking Time: 20 Minutes
Total Time: 25 Minutes

1 green plantain, peeled
1 small carrot (or 2-3 baby carrots), thinly sliced
salt and pepper to taste
½ tsp olive oil
1 slice red onion, finely chopped
1 ¾ cups water
1 cube chicken broth
1 tsp Mari's homemade seasoning
a few leaves cilantro, finely chopped

Cut plantain into thin slices (about ¼").

In a medium non-stick saucepan, bring water to a boil; add the rest of the ingredients.

Cook uncovered at medium heat until plantains are very smooth (18-20 minutes).

Serve & garnish with shredded cheese and minced red onions.

Plantain Soup

Tasty Plantain

Tasty Plantain

Serves: 1
Cooking Time: 15 Minutes
Total Time: 20 Minutes

1 green plantain, peeled, cut in three pieces
3 cups water
1 small clove garlic, minced or mashed
1 tablespoon bacon bits
½ tablespoon fresh cilantro, finely chopped
2 tablespoon olive oil
1 cube chicken broth
⅛ tablespoon salt

Bring into a boil a medium saucepan or pot with water, salt and the cube of chicken broth; reduce heat to medium-high, and add plantain. Cover and cook until plantain has softened, about 15 minutes.

Transfer the plantain to a medium size large bowl or deep plate; reserve the water. Mash plantain, adding olive oil and some of the water until smooth (about 4-6 tbsp water). Add the cilantro, bacon bits; blend and serve.

Serving suggestion: Blend together: 1 tbsp olive oil, ½ tbsp minced cilantro, pinch of salt and 1 small minced (or mashed) garlic; top plantain with oil mix.

Note: Serve immediately and eat while it's still warm (cooling will harden the mix).

Plantain in Vinaigrette

Plantain in Vinaigrette

Serves: 1
Cooking Time: 10 Minutes
Total Time: 15 Minutes

1 green plantain, peeled, cut in three pieces
3 cups water
a pinch of salt

For vinaigrette:
¼ cup olive oil
⅛ cup white vinegar
1 bay leave
1 small clove garlic, sliced
2 olives, sliced (optional)
2-3 tbsp green onions, finely sliced
6 peppercorns
a pinch of salt

Bring into a boil a medium pot with water with salt; reduce heat to medium-high, and add plantain. Cover and cook aprox 10 minutes. (don't overcook).
Drain plantain.

Prepare the vinaigrette, mixing all the ingredients; heat in microwave (medium-high heat) for about 45 seconds to blend flavors.

Cut plantain in thick slices, pour on the vinaigrette and slightly toss. Refrigerate for at least ½ hour.
Serve cold or at room temperature. You may remove the garlic, peppercorns and bay leave prior to serving.

Serve alone or as a side dish.

Healthy habits: eat well and exercise…

Dips & Spreads

My Avocado Dip-Spread with Tequila (garnished with fried plantain)

My Avocado Dip-Spread with Tequila

Serves: 1
Cooking Time: 0 Minutes
Total Time: 5 Minutes

1 small avocado, finely chopped (~ 5 oz)
½ tbsp fresh lemon juice
2 tbsp ketchup
½ tbsp olive oil
1 clove garlic, finely minced or mashed
1 tbsp cilantro, finely chopped
a pinch of salt & pepper
⅛ oz Tequila

Blend all ingredients and serve in a margarita glass with your favorite chips.

My Avocado Dip-Spread II

Serves: 1
Cooking Time: 0 Minutes
Total Time: 5 Minutes

1 avocado, small, finely chopped
½ plum tomato, finely chopped
a few leaves fresh cilantro, finely chopped
1 clove garlic, minced or mashed
⅛ cup red onions, finely chopped
⅛ cup spinach, shredded
salt and black/red /cajun pepper – to taste
1 small chili pepper – optional
1 tbsp olive oil
1 tbsp lemon juice

Toss all ingredients.

Let it stand for a few minutes to allow flavors to blend.

Serve with sliced french bread or crackers.

Tuna Dip-Spread

Serves: 1
Cooking Time: 0 Minutes
Total Time: 5 Minutes

1 can 6 oz tuna in water
1 slice red onion, chopped
1 plum tomato, chopped
1 tsp olive oil
1 tsp ketchup
salt & pepper to taste
½ avocado, finely chopped
a pinch of salt
2 tsp whole kernel corn
1 tsp green bell pepper, finely chopped

Drain tuna and blend with all the ingredients.

Serve with crackers or toasts.

Easy Seafood Dip-Spread

Serves: 1
Cooking Time: 0 Minutes
Total Time: 5 Minutes

4-6 oz cream cheese, at room temperature
1 can 6 oz crab meat
2 slices onion – finely chopped
1 tsp fresh lemon juice
a few leaves of cilantro, finely chopped
1 can 6 oz shrimp (peeled, cleaned, cooked)
a few drops of hot sauce (to taste)
cajun spice, to taste

Blend all ingredients.

Serve at room temperature with crackers or toasts.

Crab & Tuna Spread

Serves: 1
Cooking Time: 0 Minutes
Total Time: 5 Minutes

6-8 oz cream cheese, softened
a few leaves cilantro, finely chopped
1 can 6 oz crab meat, drained
1 can 6 oz tuna, drained
salt & pepper, to taste
a pinch of cajun pepper

Blend all ingredients.

Serve with crackers, toasts, or in sandwiches.

Chicken Spread with Pineapple

Serves: 1
Cooking Time: 10 Minutes
Total Time: 15 Minutes

4-6 oz chicken breast, boneless, cut into thin strips
2 cups of water
1 tbsp salt

a pinch of white sugar
1 tbsp crushed pineapple
1 tbsp red onion, finely chopped

Bring water and salt to a boil, add the chicken and simmer for about 10 minutes.

Drain, shred chicken and set aside. Allow a few minutes to cool.

Once chicken is cool (room temperature), add the rest of the ingredients and blend well.

Serve with bread or crackers.

Salsa Dip

Serves: 1
Cooking Time: 0 Minutes
Total Time: 5 Minutes

1 plum tomato, finely chopped
1 tbsp fresh lemon juice
a few leaves of cilantro, finely chopped
1 slice red onion, finely chopped
salt and pepper to taste
a pinch of sugar
1 garlic, crushed
2 slices avocado, finely chopped

Blend well all ingredients.

Cool in refrigerator for at least ½ hour to allow flavors to blend well.

Like it hot? Add a few drops of hot sauce, cajun spice, or a small chili pepper (finely chopped) to the mix.

Tuna Dip-Spread

Serves: 1
Cooking Time: 0 Minutes
Total Time: 5 Minutes

1 small tomato, chopped
1 can 4 oz tuna in water, drained
2 slices red onion – minced
2 tsp ketchup
1 tsp low-fat mayonnaise
1 tsp olive oil
a few drops of hot sauce (to taste), or a pinch of cajun spice
a few leaves spinach, chopped
a few leaves cilantro, chopped

Mix all ingredients and serve at room temperature.

Serving suggestion: serve at room temperature with crackers, toast; also great on sandwiches.

Chicken Dip-Spread

Serves: 1
Cooking Time: 0 Minutes
Total Time: 5 Minutes

1 small tomato, chopped
4-6 oz cooked chicken (boneless) – you can use canned chicken
2 slices red onion – minced
2 tsp ketchup
1 tsp low-fat mayonnaise
1 tsp olive oil
a few drops of hot sauce (to taste)
a few leaves spinach, chopped
a few leaves cilantro, chopped
2-3 slices avocado, mashed

Mix all ingredients and serve at room temperature with crackers, bread or toasts.

Beans Salad-Dip

Serves: 1
Cooking Time: 0 Minutes
Total Time: 5 Minutes

1 plum tomato, chopped
2 slices red onion, chopped
2 slices green bell pepper, chopped
a few leaves spinach, finely chopped
a few leaves cilantro, finely chopped
a pinch of dry seasonings (your preference)
⅛ cup black beans, drained
⅛ cup red kidney beans, drained
⅛ cup whole kernel corn
2 tsp white vinegar
4 tsp olive oil
1 tsp fresh lemon juice
2 slices avocado, finely chopped
a few drops of hot sauce (optional)

Toss all ingredients.

You may refrigerate or serve at room temperature.

Serving suggestion: serve as a dip with corn chips, crackers, toasts or in wraps.

Special Pink Dip-Spread

Serves: 1
Cooking Time: 0 Minutes
Total Time: 5 Minutes

4 tbsp ketchup
4 tbsp low-fat mayonnaise
1 garlic, minced or mashed
salt and pepper (red and/or black)
a few drops of hot oil, to taste (optional)
½ tsp sugar
a few leaves of cilantro, finely chopped

Mix all ingredients, whisk until mayonnaise is well blended. Serve.

Serving suggestion: Great with toasted bread, breadsticks, crackers, french fries or baked sweet potato

Note: instead of adding hot oil, you may also add hot ketchup (half and half)

Creamy Easy Dip

Serves: 1
Cooking Time: 0 Minutes
Total Time: 5 Minutes

4 tbsp low-fat mayonnaise
4 tbsp ketchup
1 tbsp Mari's homemade seasoning
½ tbsp red or black pepper
a few drops of hot oil – optional

Mix all ingredients, and serve

Serving suggestion: Great for french fries or sweet potato strips.

French Dip

Serves: 1
Cooking Time: 0 Minutes
Total Time: 5 Minutes

4 tbsp french salad dressing
1 tsp bacon bits
a few leaves spinach, finely chopped
red or black pepper, to taste

Mix all ingredients, and serve

Serving suggestion: Great for veggies, fried plantain and french fries.

Love yourself, eat well…

Stir-Fries

Stir Fry Beef over Pasta

Serves: 1
Cooking Time: 15 Minutes
Total Time: 20 Minutes

4-5 oz round steak beef, cut into thin slices (or other type of beef steak)

To marinate:
2 tbsp soy sauce
1 crushed garlic
1 tbsp olive oil
salt and pepper to taste

1 slice red onion, chopped
1 slice yellow bell pepper, chopped
1 slice green bell pepper, chopped
a few leaves of cilantro, chopped
1 small plum tomato, chopped (or a few grape tomatoes, cut in halves)

Marinate beef for at least 1 hour.

Stir-fry beef (pour all the marinade, plus 1/8 cup water) in a covered medium size non-stick frying pan at medium heat until beef is cooked (aprox 10-12 minutes)

Add the rest of the ingredients, and stir fry, uncovered, for additional 2-3 minutes, tossing occasionally.

Serve over your favorite pasta.

Quick Oriental Rice

Serves: 1
Cooking Time: 3 Minutes
Total Time: 5 Minutes

1 cup cooked rice
1 tbsp soy sauce
1 tbsp olive oil
1 egg
½ tsp olive oil (to prepare scramble)
2 slices cooked ham or turkey, cut in long thin strips
1/8 cup cabbage, shredded
1 small carrot, finely sliced
a few drops of hot sauce., to taste
a few leaves of cilantro, finely chopped

In a non-stick frying pan, pour ½ tsp oil and heat in medium-high heat.

Add egg and beat in scramble.

Then add all the rest of the ingredients, reduce heat to medium. Mix constantly for 1 minute.

Serve.

Hints: Much better if you use rice from previous day.

Shrimp Cocktail with Wine

Shrimp Cocktail with Wine

Serves: 1
Cooking Time: 2 Minutes
Total Time: 5 Minutes

4-6 oz cooked shrimp
2 tbsp white zinfandel wine
1 tbsp olive oil
1 slice green bell pepper, chopped
1 slice red onion, chopped
a few leaves cilantro, chopped
½ tsp Mari's homemade seasoning
a pinch of salt

Stir-fry all ingredients for a minute or two, at medium high-heat.

Serve in a cocktail glass, alone or as a side dish.

Stir Fry Rice, Shrimp and Veggies

Serves: 1
Cooking Time: 6-8 Minutes
Total Time: 12 Minutes

"A" ingredients:
  1 tsp soy sauce
  1-2 oz fresh broccoli, chopped
  1 slice green bell pepper, chopped
  1 slice yellow bell pepper, chopped
  1-2 oz carrots, finely sliced
  1 tsp hot sauce or ½ chili, finely chopped
  2 tsp olive oil
  ⅛ cup white wine
  1 slice red onions, chopped

"B" ingredients:
  ¼ cup cooked shrimp, cleaned, peeled
  a few leaves spinach, chopped
  1 plum tomato, chopped
  ½ cup cooked rice (white or brown), room temperature

Stir-fry ingredients in "A" in medium-high heat until veggies are tender.

Add the rest of the ingredients and stir for a couple of minutes to blend all flavors (without overcooking spinach and tomatoes).

Serve

Stir Fry Salad with Turkey Ham

Serves: 1
Cooking Time: 5 Minutes
Total Time: 10 Minutes

1 slice red onion, chopped
2 tsp olive oil
1 small plum tomato, diced
1 slice green bell pepper, finely chopped
1 clove garlic, minced or mashed
salt and pepper – to taste
3-4 oz turkey ham, cooked, diced
a few leaves fresh cilantro, finely chopped

In a frying pan, heat oil at medium-heat.

Add all ingredients, and stir constantly until veggies are tender and ham is slightly browned.

Serving suggestion: Top over rice or baked potato.

Fast food at home…

Hot Dogs, Pizza, & more...

Hot Dogs

Serves: 1
Cooking Time: 3 Minutes
Total Time: 8 Minutes

1 chicken, meat or beef hot dog
1 cup water
hot dogs bun

Topping Mix:
      1 slice avocado
      ½ tsp low-fat mayonnaise
      1 tsp red onion, finely chopped
      1 slice tomato, finely chopped
      ½ tsp olive oil
      ½ tsp ketchup (or hot ketchup)
      a pinch of salt and pepper

Cook hot dogs in boiling water for about 2 minutes. Drain well.

Place hot dog on bun.

In a mixing bowl, mix well all the topping mix ingredients.

Top hot dog with the topping mix.

Serve.

Bacon-Striped Hot Dogs

Serves: 1
Cooking Time: 3 Minutes
Total Time: 8 Minutes

1 chicken, meat or beef hot dog
1 slice bacon
hot dogs bun
melted cheese (your preference)

Wrap hot dog with the bacon strip.

Cook in toaster over until bacon starts to crisp

Place hot dog in bun

Top with melted cheese

Quickie Mini-Pizzas

Serves: 1
Cooking Time: 2 Minutes
Total Time: 5 Minutes

4-6 slices tomato, chopped
2 thin slices red onion, chopped
4-6 tbsp pizza sauce
A few leaves spinach, chopped
A few leaves fresh cilantro, chopped
4 tbsp shredded parmesan, pepperjack and/or cheddar cheese
a pinch of dry seasonings (your preference)
1-2 oz chicken, ham, shrimp or beef; cooked or broiled, finely chopped
french bread cut in halves

Top french bread halves with pizza sauce, then with the rest of the ingredients, leaving the cheese for the last.

Broil in toaster oven until cheese is melted and bread edges starts browning.

Serve and enjoy.

Baked Sweet Potato Strips

Serves: 1
Cooking Time: 15-20 Minutes
Total Time: 25 Minutes

1 sweet potato

Pre-heat conventional oven (or toaster oven) to 425°F.

Peel and cut sweet potato into thin strips.

Place strips on greased cooking sheet or shallow oven tray (greased with cooking spray); bake until cooked and tender (but crisp on the outside), about 15-20 minutes.

Serve and season immediately with salt, black & cajun pepper, to taste.

Note: No seasoning required if served with dip

King Crab Cocktail

Serves: 1
Cooking Time: 0 Minutes
Total Time: 5 Minutes

3-4 oz king crab (cooked), chopped
1 slice red onion, finely chopped
1 sliced green bell pepper, finely chopped
2 olives, finely sliced
1 slice tomato, finely chopped
2 tbsp olive oil
1 tbsp white vinegar

Mix all ingredients; allow a few minutes to blend flavors.

Serve in a glass.

Also great on crackers or fried plantain.

Sweet Carrots

Serves: 1
Cooking Time: 5 Minutes
Total Time: 8 Minutes

1 large carrot, cut diagonally, 1" thick (or 8-10 baby carrots)
olive oil or oil spray
dry seasonings
a few leaves fresh cilantro, finely chopped
1 garlic, finely chopped or mashed
1 tbsp brown sugar

In a shallow microwave-able container, spray bottom with olive oil spray and put carrots in a single layer.

Then top with cilantro, garlic and seasonings.

Sprinkle with brown sugar.

Cover and cook in medium-high for aprox 4-5 minutes (until carrots are tender).

Squared Potatoes

Serves: 1
Cooking Time: 4 Minutes
Total Time: 6 Minutes

1 potato, medium size

3 tsp olive oil
salt & pepper, to taste   } to marinate
cajun pepper, to taste

parmesan cheese, grated

Peel potato and cut into 1″ squares.

Put potatoes into plastic bag; add all the marinate ingredients and mix well.

Pour potatoes into a microwave-able bowl in a single layer.

Add all the liquid from the marinade; cover and cook in microwave oven for aprox 4 minutes or until potatoes are tender. Don't overcook.

Remove from oven and serve.

Sprinkle with parmesan cheese.

Got greens?

Salads

Avocado Salad with Chick Peas

Serves: 1
Cooking Time: 0 Minutes
Total Time: 5 Minutes

1 medium avocado
2 tsp olive oil
1 tsp white vinegar
a pinch of salt and pepper
1 tsp fresh lemon juice
a few leaves fresh cilantro, finely chopped
a few leaves spinach, finely chopped
1 slice red onion, finely chopped
2 tsp ketchup
1 garlic, minced or mashed
3-4 tsp chick peas (cooked canned chick peas, drained)

Cut avocado in half, remove the seed. Peel and set aside.

Toss all the rest of the ingredients.

Spoon the mix into the two avocado halves.

Serve.

Cabbage Salad with Avocado Dressing

Serves: 1
Cooking Time: 0 Minutes
Total Time: 5 Minutes

½ cup red cabbage, shredded
½ cup green cabbage, shredded
grated parmesan cheese

Combine red and green cabbage.

Top with avocado dressing (see recipe on this book).

Sprinkle with grated parmesan cheese

Serve

Cabbage Salad with Avocado Dressing

Chicken Salad with Beer

Chicken Salad with Beer

Serves: 1
Cooking Time: 15 Minutes
Total Time: 20 Minutes

1 chicken breast, boneless, skinless, cut into thin strips
3 tsp olive oil
1 plum tomato, chopped
2 slices red onion, chopped
2 cans of beer (12 oz each)
1 leave of lettuce, chopped
1 ½ tsp white vinegar
a few leaves spinach, chopped
a few leaves fresh cilantro, chopped
salt and pepper, to taste
dry seasonings mix

In a large saucepan, cook chicken in beer at medium-high heat until chicken is tender, about 15 minutes.

Remove from heat, drain well, and let it cool for a few minutes.

Shred chicken or cut in small chunks.

Toss with the rest of the ingredients (except spices).

Serve over a leaf of lettuce. You may serve it at room temperature or cool in the refrigerator for a few minutes before serving.

Sprinkle with spices.

Dry seasonings mix: paprika, red and black pepper, salt, garlic powder, and curry powder.

Fruity Potato Salad

Serves: 1
Cooking Time: 10 Minutes
Total Time: 15 Minutes

7-8 oz potatoes, peeled and cut in 1-inch squares
3 cups water
1 tsp salt
2 tbsp low-fat mayonnaise
⅛ cup apple, peeled and cut into 1-inch squares
⅛ cup pear, peeled and cut into 1-inch squares

In a medium-large saucepan or pot, bring water to a boil.

Add the salt and potatoes. Reduce heat to medium-low and simmer until potatoes are tender (don't overcook), aprox 8-10 minutes.

Drain and set aside to cool down.

Transfer potatoes to medium size bowl; add the rest of the ingredients, toss and Serve.

It can be served cold or at room temperature.

Double Potato Salad

Serves: 1
Cooking Time: 10 Minutes
Total Time: 15 Minutes

6 oz potatoes, cut in 1-inch squares
6 oz sweet potatoes, cut in 1-inch squares
3 cups water
1 tsp salt
1 cube chicken flavor
a few leaves of fresh cilantro, finely chopped
1 garlic, minced or mashed
1 slice of red onion, finely chopped
salt and fresh ground pepper – to taste

To garnish:
green onions, thinly sliced
red bell pepper, finely chopped
1 slice of tomato, finely chopped

In a medium-large saucepan or pot, bring water to a boil. Add the cube of chicken flavor, salt and potatoes. Reduce heat to medium-low and simmer until potatoes are tender (don't overcook), aprox 8-10 minutes.

Drain potatoes (reserve ¼ cup of liquid).

Fold in the cilantro, red onions, olive oil, and garlic. You may add some of the liquid to get the right consistency. Add salt and pepper to taste. Mix should be smooth, but still chunky.

Serve and garnish with green onions, red bell pepper, and tomatoes.

Green and Red Salad

Serves: 1
Cooking Time: 0 Minutes
Total Time: 5 Minutes

¼ cup romaine lettuce
¼ cup red leaf lettuce
¼ cup baby spinach
1 plum tomato, thinly sliced
1 slice red onion, thinly sliced
1 slice red bell pepper, chopped
1 slice green bell pepper, chopped

Manually shred lettuces and spinach.

Toss the rest of the ingredients.

Serve

Serving suggestion: Top with grated parmesan cheese and vinaigrette dressing.

Veggie Potato Salad

Serves: 1
Cooking Time: 10 Minutes
Total Time: 20 Minutes

2 medium potatoes, peeled, cut into 1-inch cubes
1 tsp salt
3 tsp low-fat mayonnaise
fresh ground pepper –to taste
½ carrot, shredded
¼ cup broccoli, finely chopped
1 hard-boiled egg, peeled, finely chopped
a few leaves fresh cilantro, finely chopped
1 small plum tomato, finely chopped
1 slice red onions, finely chopped
1 slice green bell peppers, finely chopped
4-5 leaves baby spinach, shredded

Bring into a boil a medium pot with water and salt. Reduce to medium heat, add the potatoes, and cook until potatoes are still firm but tender, about 10 minutes.

Meanwhile, chop and shred the rest of the ingredients.

Drain well and transfer to a large bowl. Let stand for 5 minutes to cool down a little bit.

Add the rest of the ingredients, and toss to combine.

Serve

Note: to save time, you may boil the eggs with the potatoes. Add them to the water while still cold to prevent cracking.

Bean Tuna Salad

Serves: 1
Cooking Time: 0 Minutes
Total Time: 5 Minutes

¾ to 1 cup mixed beans (canned cooked beans), drained
        red kidney beans
        black beans
        garbanzo beans
        pinto beans
1 slice red onion
a few drops fresh lemon juice
salt and pepper, to taste
1 tsp olive oil
½ tsp white vinegar
3-4 oz tuna (canned, drained)
1 slice tomato, chopped
a few leaves spinach, chopped
a few leaves fresh cilantro, chopped

In a mixing bowl, combine all ingredients and toss to blend.

Serve.

Penne Pasta Salad

Serves: 1
Cooking Time: 8-10 Minutes
Total Time: 15 Minutes

2-3 oz penne pasta
2 cups water
a pinch of salt

about 1 oz of each of these veggies:
      sliced carrots
      whole kernel corn
      red and green bell-peppers
2 slices tomato, chopped
a few leaves spinach, chopped
1-2 oz avocado, chopped
1 clove garlic, mashed
salt and pepper, to taste
2 tsp olive oil
1 tsp balsamic vinegar
a few drops fresh lemon juice

Cook pasta in water and salt for 8-10 minutes. Drain and set aside to cool.

In a large mixing bowl, combine all the rest of the ingredients and toss well. Add pasta and toss.

Serve.

Warm-Me-Up Soup…

Soup

Rooty Soup

Rooty Soup

Serves: 1-2
Cooking Time: 25-30 Minutes
Total Time: 35 Minutes

2-3 oz chicken breast, cut into 1-inch cubes or thinly strips
2-3 oz shrimp, peeled and cleaned
a few leaves of fresh cilantro, chopped
1 clove garlic, minced or mashed
¼ cup sweet potato, peeled, diced
¼ cup potato, peeled, diced
¼ cup squash, peeled, diced
¼ cup plantain (green), peeled, thinly sliced
salt and black/red pepper – to taste
3 cups water
½ small plum tomato, finely chopped
1 tsp Mari's homemade seasoning
1 cube chicken broth

Bring water to a boil in a large saucepan or pot.

Add chicken and cook at med-high heat until chicken is cooked, about 15 minutes.

Add the rest of the ingredients and cook for additional 10-15 minutes until vegetables are fully cooked (don't over cook). Stir occasionally.

Serve.

Note: Save time – cut vegetables and prepare the rest of the ingredients while you cook the chicken.

Beef, Meat & Chicken

Easy Ground Beef with Veggies

Easy Ground Beef with Veggies

Serves: 1
Cooking Time: 20 Minutes
Total Time: 30 Minutes

4-6 oz lean ground beef (ground chicken, turkey or meat)
2 tbsp water
1 tbsp olive oil
salt and pepper, to taste
¾ cup of mixed veggies (peas, corn, and carrots), fresh or frozen
a few leaves fresh cilantro, chopped
1 tsp Mari's homemade seasoning

Season the ground beef with the salt and pepper.

In a medium non-stick saucepan or frying pan, add the water, oil, Mari's homemade seasoning and the beef. Cook covered, at medium-high heat until well done, about 15-20 minutes. Stir occasionally.

Once cooked, add the veggies and cilantro. Check again for salt and pepper, toss and cook (covered) for additional 5 minutes at medium heat.

Serve.

Chicken My Style

Serves: 1
Cooking Time: 25 Minutes
Total Time: 30 Minutes

1 chicken breast, boneless, skinless, cut into thin strips
4 tbsp olive oil
2 tbsp white vinegar
Salt and pepper, to taste
1 white onion, in thick slices
1 green bell pepper, in thick slices
2 bay leaves
¼ cup water

Marinate chicken in olive oil, vinegar, garlic, salt and pepper for a few hours (preferably overnight).

In a medium size frying pan, pour chicken with all its liquid.

Add the water, onions, bell pepper, and bay leaves.

Cook covered at medium-low heat until chicken is tender, about 20 minutes; stirring occasionally.

Then cook for additional 5 minutes, uncovered, at medium-high to evaporate most of the liquid.

You don't need to be an Italian to love pasta…

Pasta

Stuffed Pasta Shells

Serves: 1
Cooking Time: 25 Minutes
Total Time: 30 Minutes

4 oz cream cheese, softened
3-4 oz crab meat and/or shrimps, cooked
1 tsp green onions finely sliced
salt and pepper, to taste
a few leaves fresh cilantro, finely chopped
5-6 jumbo pasta shells
2 cups water
4-6 tsp spaghetti sauce
shredded or grated parmesan cheese

Bring water to a boil, add salt and pasta shells; simmer aprox 10 minutes, don't over cook. Drain and set aside to cool.

Mix cream cheese, crab meat and/or shrimp, green onions, salt, pepper and cilantro.

Stuff pasta shells with cream cheese mix and put it into a non-stick oven casserole. Top with spaghetti sauce, sprinkle with cheese.

Place into toaster oven at 375° for about 15 minutes or until cheese is melted.

Tortelloni with Vinaigrette Sauce

Tortelloni with Vinaigrette Sauce

Serves: 1
Cooking Time: 8 Minutes
Total Time: 13 Minutes

Pasta:
4 oz chicken and prosciutto tortelloni
1 ½ cup water
a pinch of salt

Sauce:
2 tbsp olive oil
1 tbsp balsamic vinegar
1 slice red onion, chopped
4-6 grape tomatoes, cut in halves
a few leaves fresh cilantro
1 clove garlic, minced
1 slice green bell pepper, chopped
salt and pepper, to taste

Bring water to a boil in a large saucepan or pot, add salt and pasta. Reduce heat to medium-low and cook for 8 minutes.

Drain pasta and set aside.

To prepare the sauce: In a small saucepan, mix all ingredients for the sauce and heat for 1 minute at medium heat to blend flavors.

Top pasta with sauce, and serve.

Eggs

Ham and Veggie Omelet

Serves: 1
Cooking Time: 10 Minutes
Total Time: 15 Minutes

1 small potato, thinly sliced
1 tsp olive oil
1 tsp butter

Eggs mix:
2 slightly beaten eggs
1 slice of cooked ham, finely chopped
1 slice of red onion, finely chopped
2 slices of tomato, finely chopped
1 slice green bell pepper, finely chopped
salt and pepper to taste

In a small size frying pan, at medium heat, hot oil and butter; add potatoes to cover the bottom of the pan. Cook in low heat until potatoes are tender, aprox 2-3 minutes each side.

In the meantime, prepare egg mix.

Once potatoes are tender, add the eggs mix and let it cook thoroughly at low heat, flip once.

Serve.

Serving suggestion: Serve with sliced french bread. Garnish with low-fat bacon bits.

Gourmet Eggs

Serves: 1
Cooking Time: 7 Minutes
Total Time: 12 Minutes

3 eggs, hard boiled

½ tsp mayonnaise, low-fat
½ tsp dijon mustard
a few drops of hot sauce – optional
1 slice of tomato, finely chopped
1 small garlic, mashed
a few leaves of fresh cilantro, finely chopped
½ tsp bacon bits
salt and fresh ground pepper to taste

Cook eggs in a medium size saucepan with water for about 7 minutes, drain and set aside to cool down.

Peel and cut eggs in half (lengthwise), and scoop out the egg yolks.

Mix egg yolks with the rest of the ingredients.

Stuff egg whites with mixture.

Sprinkle with salt and pepper to taste

Serving suggestion: Great as appetizer, breakfast or side dish.

Because sometimes you just want something sweet…

Drinks & Sweets...

Cottage Cheese with Tangerines

Cottage Cheese with Tangerines

Serves: 1
Cooking Time: 0 Minutes
Total Time: 8 Minutes

3-4 oz cottage cheese, chilled

To prepare Syrup:
    1 ½ tangerine orange, peeled
    2 tsp sugar (or substitute)
    8-10 pistachios, peeled

To garnish:
    8-10 pistachios, peeled
    ½ tangerine orange, peeled
    powdered sugar

In an electric blender, blend the tangerine, pistachios and the sugar to get a syrup consistency. Mix well and taste, and add more sugar if needed, to your taste.

Serve cottage cheese and top with the syrup.

Garnish with tangerine and pistachios.

Sprinkle with powdered sugar.

Note: you may substitute tangerines for fresh peaches or strawberries.

Strawberry Pancake

Strawberry Pancake

Serves: 1
Cooking Time: 4-5 Minutes
Total Time: 8 Minutes

pancake mix (just-add-water mix), low fat
1-2 strawberries, finely chopped

pancake syrup, low fat, strawberry flavored

To garnish:
 cinnamon
 powdered sugar
 1-2 strawberries

Prepare the pancake mix (1-2 pancakes) per box instructions; whisk to blend thoroughly. Mix should be smooth, not too thick.

Coat a non-stick skillet with cooking spray (butter flavored), and pre-heat over medium heat.

Pour ¾ of the mix in the skillet to form a pancake, top with strawberries, then with the rest of the pancake mix. Cook at low heat, flipping only once. About 2 minutes each side.

Serve.

Top with syrup, cinnamon, powdered sugar and strawberries.

Soda-Cream Shake

Serves: 1
Cooking Time: 0 Minutes
Total Time: 5 Minutes

2 scoops vanilla ice cream*
1 can soda (cola)

Go for low-fat ingredients for lower calories

In a blender, mix the ingredients until smooth.

Serve in a tall glass with drinking straw.

*Add more ice-cream for a thicker shake.

Serving suggestion: Top with (low sugar) whipped cream.

Fruity Yogurt Dessert

Serves: 1
Cooking Time: 0 Minutes
Total Time: 5 Minutes

3 strawberries, sliced
6 tsp low-fat strawberry yogurt, chilled
4 tsp whip cream, chilled
½ banana, sliced
2 tsp white coconut, shredded

In a dessert glass, layer the ingredients in the following order:

3 tsp yogurt, 2 sliced strawberries, 2 tsp whip cream, 1 tsp coconut, 3 tsp yogurt, sliced banana, 2 tsp whip cream. Sprinkle with coconut.

Serving suggestion: Garnish with one sliced strawberry.

Caramelized Fruits on Ice Cream

Caramelized Fruits on Ice Cream

Serves: 1
Cooking Time: 0 Minutes
Total Time: 5 Minutes

3 tsp butter
3 tsp brown sugar
½ small banana, thickly sliced
1-2 slices pear (or in chunks)
2-3 scoops low-fat ice cream or frozen yogurt
cinnamon powder
½ oz Irish cream (liquor)
whip cream – optional

In a non-stick frying pan, at medium heat, melt the butter, add the sugar and Irish cream and stir to get a syrup consistency.

Toss in the fruits and cook for additional ~30 seconds (blend flavors without breaking up the fruits). Set aside.

Serve ice cream; pour caramelized fruits on top.

Sprinkle with cinnamon. Top with whip cream (optional)

Eat immediately, it will melt <u>very</u> fast.

Fruity Shake

Fruity Shake

Serves: 1
Cooking Time: 0 Minutes
Total Time: 5 Minutes

1 banana, peeled
3-4 oz low-fat milk
3-4 fresh strawberries
½ cup crushed ice
2 scoops low-fat ice cream, yogurt or sorbet – strawberry flavored
1 tsp sugar or substitute

Chunk fruits and blend with the rest of the ingredients until smooth.

Serve on tall glass.

Great for breakfast or snack time.

Champola Shake

Serves: 1
Cooking Time: 0 Minutes
Total Time: 5 Minutes

2/3 cup evaporated milk (or low-fat evaporated milk)
2/3 cup guava juice
1 cup crushed ice
a few drops fresh lemon juice
2 tsp sugar (or substitute)

In an electric blender, blend well all ingredients to get a thick shake.

Serve in a tall glass.

Champola Shake

Easy Flavored Coffee

Easy Flavored Coffee

Serves: 1
Cooking Time: 0 Minutes
Total Time: 5 Minutes

2/3 cup low-fat milk
2 tsp coffee creamer
freshly brewed coffee, about 1/3 cup
1 tsp brown sugar (or substitute)
cinnamon
¼ oz crème de cacao, to taste

Brew coffee as you normally do.

In the meantime, pour milk and coffee creamer in a big mug, and heat on microwave until it starts to boil, watch it doesn't overflow. Remove immediately.

Add sugar to the milk. Using the electric mixer, blend the milk to get a thick foamy consistency.

In a coffee mug or glass, pour the coffee, crème de cacao, and add the milk very slowly, holding the foam as this should go on the top (use a spoon to hold the foam).

Scoop the milk foam on top and sprinkle with cinnamon.

Note: adjust amount of milk and black coffee to get desired coffee taste and color. Adjust liquor (crème de cacao) to your taste.

Creamy Fruit Shake

Serves: 1
Cooking Time: 0 Minutes
Total Time: 5 Minutes

1 cup of mixed frozen fruits (papaya, strawberries, banana, pineapple) *
2 scoops lowfat vanilla ice cream
1 cup lowfat milk
a pinch of cinnamon
2 drops of vanilla extract
1 tbsp sugar or substitute

In a blender, mix all ingredients.

Add ice cream, one scoop at a time until you get the desired thickness.

* Fruits should be frozen, cut in chunks. You may use a mix of 2 or more fruits.

I hope you've enjoyed the recipes of this book!

- *Mari*

Mari lives in Hillsboro, Oregon since 1999. She lives with her son, Dennis.